NIBBLE YOUR WAY TO SUCCESS

56 Winning Tips for Taking Charge of Your Career

Nan S. Russell

MountainWorks Press

Published by MountainWorks Press
PO Box 1327
Whitefish, MT 59937
info@MountainWorksPress.com

ISBN-13: 978-0-9792802-0-7
ISBN-10:   0-9792802-0-6

Printed in the United States of America

Table of Contents

Why this Book? 1

Impressions 4

Become Absorbed 7

It's Not the Idea 8

Not Motivated to Work? Bored? Tired? 9

Keep Paddling 10

There Is No Secret 11

Increase Your Altitude 12

Head *and* Heart 13

Think Smorgasbord 14

Remember What It's Like 16

Give What's Missing 17

The Trust Mirror 19

Serve Your Politics Well 21

You're Contagious 22

Pull Weeds of Self-Doubt 24

Don't Listen to Naysayers 25

It's Not About Time 27

Get Your Day's Worth 30

Understand Deadlines 31

Work Should Not Be Work 32

The Work that Makes Us Happy 33

Stop the Gnawing 34

Learn to Nibble 35

Think in Parallel 37

Immoveable Deadlines 39

Finding Time 41

Keeping Work in Perspective 43

Take It or Leave It ... But Get It 44

Live and Learn Days 45

Step Out 46

You Have to Be Out There 48

Ideas In – Ideas Out 50

Check Your Thoughts 51

Power Your Future 54

Watch Yourself 56

Read the Tea Leaves 58

Find People Touchstones 59
Like What You Do..60
Tell 'Em Why..61
How Many Minds Have You Read Today? 62
Show, Don't Tell 63
Schedule Self-Appointments 64
Clean Sweep Those Inner Files..65
Assess Your Progress...66
One Idea a Day..68
Become A Quotation Lover 70
Invest in You...72
Learn to Write..73
Put Your Name to Your Work 74
Learn and Practice Your Craft 75
Pay Attention to Little Things on Your Resume 76
Don't Even Think About Pushing SEND!..77
Changing Rules 78
The Credit Doesn't Matter..81
What You Know, When You Know It..82
Deliver...83
It's Not the Drum 84
Take a Time Out..86
Progress, Not Perfection..88
What Can You Do for Me Today? 90
Someone Else...91

INTRODUCTION

Why this Book?

Since June 2004, I've been writing a biweekly career insights column called *Winning at Working*. In it, I share work insights and tips I learned the hard way, in the hopes that doing so might be helpful to readers. Today, thousands of subscribers get my eColumn and more than eighty publications carry *Winning at Working*.

But, it was the results of a reader survey that prompted me to expand beyond my column. Through the survey I discovered the most articulated work problems were related to something called, *not enough*. Not enough time, not enough resources, not enough people, not enough training, not enough leadership – you get the picture.

It got me thinking. What could I share? What could I do to help? Or possibly, what could I do to inspire others to consider their work challenges from a different or a new perspective?

So, I decided to write this little book. I learned in twenty years in management it's often the simple things that make a big difference in the workplace.

Nibble Your Way to Success: 56 Winning Tips for Taking Charge of Your Career is a collection of real-world, proven career insights and tips that you can use right now to make a career difference. And since I'm a quotation lover, you'll find a few of my favorites sprinkled in.

I wrote *Nibble Your Way to Success* as a way to pass insights from one person to the next, in the hopes that something I share may help you be successful at your work, whatever that is. The tips are quick and easy to digest. You can read them individually, or a couple at a time; when you need a burst of inspiration or a different way of thinking about a familiar problem.

But, I have one recommendation. Use what you like and throw away the rest. I'm not suggesting this is the answer, the only way or even the right way. All I know is that these concepts worked for me in my career, and, they've worked for hundreds of others, too. If you find *Nibble Your Way to Success* helpful, there's more winning at working philosophies and insights at www.winningatworking.com.

You'll find the phrase, "winning at working," throughout this book. It's a key philosophy for nibbling your way to success. When you offer your uniqueness, the best of who you are at the core level, to your work, you are winning at working. A winning philosophy differs from a win philosophy. If you win, it implies someone else loses. But, winning is different. Everyone can be winning. And when we're all winning, we all win.

I can't take sole credit for this book. It wouldn't have happened without the encouragement, help and support of my husband, Dan Russell; or the shepherding and tweaking of my friend, Beth Pelkofsky; or the belief challenges and nudges of my Quantum Leap coach, Steve Harrison. Thank you.

I've nibbled my way to actualizing a life-dream to live and work from the mountains of Montana; nibbled my way to starting businesses, achieving financial security, realizing goals and inventing the life I want to live. I don't know what success is for you. For me, it's becoming who I am capable of becoming, and while I'm a work in progress, I do know the way to get there is by nibbling.

Whatever your dreams and aspirations, you can nibble your way to the success you want in your life, too.

Nan Russell

ഔഔഔ

"Nobody can contribute to the best of humanity who does not make the best out of himself."
~ Johann Gottfried Herder ~

INSIGHT

Impressions

Even now, months after it happened, it surprises me when I think about it. No phone call. No heads up. No discussion. As I opened the email from a business associate, checking my messages from an airport lounge, I expected a routine update. Instead, I read a message severing our relationship.

What startled me wasn't that this person decided it best to change a business situation. These things happen. It was how she informed me of her decision that brought the pain. You see, it's not just what you do that matters, it's how you do it.

I discovered more about her in that instant than I had in the months we worked together. I learned she took the easy way over the right way, lacked relationship courage, and retreated from difficult encounters. Her intention was to sever the current working relationship, but in the process she also severed my respect. You see, *how* you do what you do speaks volumes about who you are and what you value. It's a telling impression that leaves an imprint on those you touch.

Sure, it's easier to use email to terminate relationships, deliver bad news or launch print-grenades. Just like it's easier to give advice when you don't have to live with the results; give orders you don't have to follow; and point out flaws you don't have to fix. And it's easier to be reactive instead of proactive, trade long-term sustained results for short-term gains and tell your boss what he wants to hear instead of what he needs to know.

All these things are easier. But easier isn't better, and easier won't get you winning at working results. Choosing the right way will. But that means finding the courage to pick up the phone and have the unpleasant conversation, terminate a relationship that's not working or deal with conflict in honest ways. It means confronting issues, being hands-on as needed and letting your life's actions speak to who you are.

I find people who are winning at working don't take the easy way, even when the right way is difficult or fear producing. *How* they do their work is as important to them as what they do. And while we all slip at how we do our work at times, out of anger or frustration, people who are winning at working know when they've slipped and keep striving to do better.

You see, the impressions we make by how we go about our work, last. Bad impressions can destroy trust, eliminate respect and derail careers. But good impressions can create trust, earn respect and build your career. Sometimes you may not like the decision, but you still respect how someone executed it. That's a good impression. Want to be winning at working and nibble your way to success? Choose the *right* way to do what you need to do, not the easy way.

TIP #1

Become Absorbed

Thomas Edison said, "The first requisite for success is the ability to apply your physical and mental energies to one problem incessantly without growing weary." And while I believe Edison is right, in this IM world, we are constantly bombarded by instant messages, emails, text messages and cell phone calls. All seek to pull our energies to other thoughts.

So, we've become good at multi-tasking. But one key to winning at working is to know when it's time to stop multi-tasking and start single-tasking.

The ability to become engaged and absorbed by your work separates people who are winning at working from those who aren't. Some call it focus. Whatever you call it, you need it. Tasking is not doing. Real doing requires absorption.

৯৯৯

TIP #2

It's Not the Idea

As a conference attendee, I was struck by the people frenzy trying to grab hold of the next big idea.

As if getting the perfect idea was going to change their success outcome or business results.

But the missing link is not having an idea, it's executing it. That's where most people flounder. They have plenty of ideas, chasing new ones, brainstorming what can be done. But, they never get around to doing them.

People who are winning at working do. They have plenty of ideas, too, but they do something about them.

એ એ એ

TIP #3

Not Motivated to Work? Bored? Tired?

Not in the mood to work today? We've all been there. How do you motivate yourself when you're not?

Do something. Anything.

Start something small that you can easily complete. Find something on your to-do list that you can accomplish quickly. Do a series of quick hitters.

I find that once I've flexed my doing-muscles, I'm ready to tackle something else and that tired, bored feeling dissipates. It's like exercising. Once I go for a walk, I get into walking and start to enjoy the feeling of moving and doing something for my body. Work is like that.

TIP #4

Keep Paddling

Canoeing on a remote wilderness lake, we passed a family in kayaks heading back toward camp. I overheard the younger of two boys telling his father that he was "too tired" to paddle.

On our return, 13 miles and four hours later, I knew what he meant. It was tiring to keep paddling. But in order to reach the shore, there wasn't a choice. So, paddle we did.

Dreams and goals and careers are like that canoe trip. Just when you're too tired, too discouraged or too overwhelmed to keep going, you need to find the strength to trudge on. It's when you want to give up that you need to keep going.

You see, it's up to you to get where you want to go in life. You're the one with the paddle. Rest when you need too, but keep paddling!

TIP #5

There Is No Secret

People are looking for the secret to success; the secret to being a millionaire; the secret to winning at working. And here's the secret - there is no secret.

People who are winning at working know it takes persistence, determination, commitment, passion, practice, focus and hard work. Success happens a step at a time.

Quit looking out there for the secret to winning at working. Look inside and you'll find everything you need.

TIP #6

Increase Your Altitude

"The hardest thing to see is what is in front of your eyes." Johann Wolfgang von Goethe.

When things go awry increase your altitude and take another look.

When you're mired in the details and lose sight of why you're doing what you're doing, increase your altitude and look again.

When you've had one of those "I wish I could quit" days, increase your altitude and consider the thought in the big scheme of what really matters in life.

People who are winning at working increase their vantage point to gain perspective. Increasing altitude increases your options, reduces stress and enhances problem-solving.

TIP #7

Head *and* Heart

Those who think the workplace is not a place for heart are wrong, in my thinking. It takes both head *and* heart to make the best decisions and to be winning at working.

As Fyodor Dostoyevsky put it: "It is not the brains that matter most, but that which guides them – the character, the heart, the generous qualities, progressive ideas."

When you use more than your head at work, you have an advantage. If you want better results, put your feelings, impressions, values and authentic self into the mix. And when my head and heart are in conflict, heart usually wins.

TIP #8

Think Smorgasbord

We have different likes and dislikes. We can watch the same movie, read the same book, eat the same food and have distinctly different reactions.

If you follow someone in line at a smorgasbord, when you get to the checkout you'll find their food selection differs from yours. And while you both might have salads, the kind of lettuce, toppings and dressing you select are unique to your tastes, mood and needs. Likewise for them.

So why are we surprised at work when bosses, clients, coworkers or staff like what we do and others don't? How can we get praise from one person and critique from another and it's the same work? Why do some people love your idea and others fight against it? Think smorgasbord.

When I get a bruised ego because someone doesn't like what I've done or what I'm suggesting, I find it helps to "think smorgasbord." This simple thought offers me perspective.

You see, we all have different experiences, different "eyes," different skills, different knowledge and different goals. These lead to different preferences and conclusions.

Just like I don't feel personally attached to what someone chooses on their dinner tray, I've learned to understand work likes and dislikes in a similar manner. Try thinking smorgasbord the next time you encounter mixed messages coming your way.

ഴഴഴ

"We don't see things as they are; we see things as we are."
~ Anais Nin ~

TIP #9

Remember What It's Like

People who are winning at working remember what it's like to be a new employee, an entry level staff member, or an idealistic first manager. They remember what it's like to feel deflated, dejected, or discouraged by something that happened at work. They remember what it's like to feel pressure and stress and confusion. And because they remember, they act towards others at work with insight, understanding and support.

When we remember what it's like, we resist thinking we're better, smarter or more talented. We stay grounded in our humanity, tied to our compassionate nature and resist the pull of power. When we remember what it's like, we become the better manager, the engaged leader or the involved parent. And when we remember what it's like, we communicate with both understanding and insight.

TIP #10

Give What's Missing

If everyone is shouting, what's missing is quiet reason.

If everyone is pointing fingers, what's missing is accountability.

If everyone is finding fault, what's missing is praise and recognition.

If everyone is in agreement, what's missing is another perspective.

If everyone is focused on short-term gains, what's missing is long-term thinking.

If everyone is thinking about their department, what's missing is thinking about the company.

If everyone is cutting corners, what's missing is quality results.

If everyone is focused on what to do, what's missing is how to do it.

If everyone is afraid to speak up, what's missing is the courage to find your voice.

If everyone is being like everyone, what's missing is
   being yourself.

   People who are winning at working offer what's
missing. They bring balance, perspective, courage and
insight to their work.

TIP #11

The Trust Mirror

As much as we like to think trust is about those people who are our bosses and coworkers, or those leaders, politicians and celebrities whose mistruths and misdeeds fill our websites and newspapers, it's also about us. As Peter Block said, "Whatever we see from our leaders can ultimately only be found in the mirror."

Most of us use the word trust loosely. Some use it as a substitute for "reliable" or "predictable" or "trustworthy." Others use it as a synonym for "confidential" or "competent." People bring experiences and baggage to the workplace and these influence their perspective. Hence, people mean different things when they use the word trust and have differing beliefs on what it is and isn't.

But most agree trust is an important component at work. When it's missing, it's noticeable in many ways. Productivity, discretionary effort and results being three. Passion, enthusiasm and engagement being six.

Creativity, energy and communication being nine. You get the point.

But here's the bottom line on trust. It's a mirror. Trust is not about them giving it to us. Trust is an action we can take. And we *start* trust by *giving* trust.

ༀༀༀ

TIP #12

Serve Your Politics Well

Politics can be served with a negative or a positive impact. It's the intention behind an action that determines whether it creates fear or builds relationships. What's the motive? If politics is a dirty word where you work, undermining results and reducing staff engagement, consider your contribution to that culture.

The politics label can be assigned to assisting other departments, supporting company initiatives, cooperating with those in charge, sharing information, and helping others achieve results. You see, strategic alignments, interdepartmental collaboration and volunteering for additional work assignments are politics, too.

Politics are not inherently good or bad. It's what's behind them. How we serve our own politics at work is a direct result of how we show up, in the deepest sense, as a person. Want to be winning at working? Serve your politics with well-meaning intention.

TIP #13

You're Contagious

Ever had a great day ruined by a coworker, boss or family member who was in a bad mood? Someone operating with a victim-mind-set or a short fuse? You know those days when everything is going well and you run across that irritable, grumpy, angry person and somehow their mood gets to yours.

But more than moods are contagious. Behavior is too, especially in the workplace. Your anger, frustration or poor example can rub off on others, too. Of course, so can your passion, enthusiasm and high standards.

If you want to be winning at working, think of your words and actions like germs. They're highly infectious. Model contagious behaviors that ignite and fuel the best in yourself and others, and you'll be amazed at the result.

କ୍ଷକ୍ଷକ୍ଷ

*"As we let our own light shine, we unconsciously give
other people permission to do the same."*
~ Marianne Williamson ~

TIP #14

Pull Weeds of Self-Doubt

It's easy to let them grow ... even thrive. You know the ones. Those voices inside your head that discourage you, berate you, planting seeds of not-sure or not-enoughness that germinate, beginning a garden of self-doubt in your head.

Like any weed, the weed of self-doubt is fast growing. Left alone it can over take a garden of good ideas, motivation, positive thinking and initiative. Your task is to stomp it out. Pull it out. Don't let it grow. Get rid of it as soon as its ugly head pops through, causing you second thoughts about your dreams or aspirations or abilities.

ళుళుళు

TIP #15

Don't Listen to Naysayers

Don't give other people power over your dreams, ambitions or future.

It's hard to sustain your energy when people around you are pulling you down. But, unless you want to be where they are, resist that pull. Just because something has been someone else's experience, doesn't mean it will be yours.

Thoughts determine reality. If you think you won't get that job or won't succeed in life, you probably won't. But you can decide you're in charge of your dreams and destiny, and you can embrace opportunities. When you do, you'll find an entirely different experience.

Remember, it's your life, not anyone else's. Life can be hard, finding a job can be hard, starting a business can be hard, doing well can be hard. But, so what? Not doing those things and losing your dreams and enthusiasm takes its toll and is hard, too.

Don't listen to the naysayers. Make up your mind that you're in charge of your future. Begin with small steps to make what you want happen.

৯১৯১৯

"If you refuse to accept anything but the best out of life, you very often get it."
~ W. Somerset Maugham ~

INSIGHT

It's Not About Time

With mounting to-do lists, big projects with short time frames, consuming workloads, growing obligations and festering unfinished tasks, it's no wonder in this what-have-you-done-for-me-today world we often feel time deprived. Work-life flows to home-life, balance becomes imbalance, and goals and dreams get relegated to a closet shelf.

If this sounds familiar, you're not alone. In a recent *Winning at Working* reader survey, the most commonly articulated work problem was related to time. Overwhelmed. Overworked. Overstressed. Too much to do and too little time to do it.

But here's the reality. No matter how much we do, we will never get everything done. There isn't enough time for all that needs doing, all we want to do or we'd like to do or we should do. There never will be, even with the most sophisticated productivity, organizational and time-management approaches. Sure, they're helpful, but thinking the chaos and stress in life is caused by not having enough time is an error.

You see, the problem is not a time problem. We all have the same amount. It's a choice problem. The choices you make determine whether you're running your life, or your life is running you. And you do have choices. Sure, there may be consequences to saying no, establishing boundaries or reordering priorities. But there are also consequences if you don't.

All tasks are not equal. All commitments are not equal. All responsibilities are not equal. All clients are not equal. All people of personal importance to your life are not equal. Yet many of us operate as if they were. You can do fifty things today and get little, if any, result for having done them. Or you can do one or two that bring a big return, be it emotional, financial, physical or psychological. People who are winning at working know the difference and operate accordingly.

They see time as life's currency and how it's used as a choice. Choices shape your results and your life. You get the same twenty-four hours each day as your co-worker down the hall. But use differs. Practice the piano eight hours a day and you'll be better than people who don't. Practice and hone your workplace talents and the same applies. Or spend time getting ready to work, shooting the breeze, surfing the web, fiddling with email and you'll complete the day having traded your time for minimal results.

How you spend your time puts value on what you're spending it on. For years, I never had "time" to exercise consistently until a health issue caused me to re-prioritize my choices. Funny how I managed to find the hours when I had to. Choosing to eliminate an hour of television created 365 "found" hours a year. That's nine work weeks.

People who are winning at working know this secret: there is always time for what matters to them. So, they allocate their time carefully, understanding their life as a reflection of their choices. They make time for the people they love, the passions they have and work that uses their uniqueness. They focus on the results, goals, and life-dreams they desire, rather than accepting what comes their way. They do, while others talk of doing. They plan their day, while others let their day plan them. And they motivate themselves, while others wait for someone or something to motivate them. For people who are winning at working, it's not about the time they have; it's about the choices they make in how to use it.

TIP #16

Get Your Day's Worth

Look around. You get the same 525,600 minutes a year everyone else gets. Yet there are people who make more progress in a month than others do in a year. There are people who seem to manifest their goals and dreams and potential while others languish in overwhelmedness.

What's the difference? One gets through the day, while the other gets their day's worth.

People who are winning at working know the difference between being busy and making progress, between doing work and adding value, between need to dos and nice to dos, and between finishing tasks and creating opportunities. They know the biggest asset they have is their time. Hence they invest it carefully, looking to maximize the return on investment.

TIP #17

Understand Deadlines

If you don't file your tax return on April 15th, there's a penalty. The same is true at work, but it's not as obvious.

If you miss a work deadline, the next time an assignment is due, extra time may be built in so your boss or colleague has what they need when they need it. These built-ins limit your future flexibility and create a credibility deficit for you.

If you want to be winning at working you need all the flexibility and credibility you can get. Meeting deadlines is one way to get both.

TIP #18

Work Should Not Be Work

"You never achieve real success unless you like what you are doing." Dale Carnegie.

If your work *is* work, think again about what you should be or could be doing. We all have times when we've had a bad day (or week) or dislike something happening in the work environment. But those times should be temporary and occasional. Consider on average, how's it going?

I use a 51% rule. If on average, at least 51% of the time I enjoy going to work and like the work I do, then I'm moving forward. When it's less than that, it's time to change course.

TIP #19

The Work that Makes Us Happy

While cleaning up my office and sorting through the scraps of newspaper clippings and articles I save for various projects and ideas, I stopped at a quotation: "You have to work ... to be happy. You're not going to get it through your career, money, or even love of another person. It's between you and yourself." Rufus Wainwright, Musician.

You can read this quotation any way you want. But, it sparked a thought in me, which of course, is what I love about quotes. As an aside, if you're a quote lover too, or looking for daily motivation, you may be interested in learning how to get yours as a DailyVitamin subscriber at www.dailyworkvitamin.com.

Anyway, here's where that spark took me. We all have unique talents, abilities, "gifts." Only when we discover what they are and offer them to the world do we become who we are. There's a difference between *doing* and *being*. That's the work that makes us happy ... *becoming* who we are.

TIP #20

Stop the Gnawing

Need to do. Have to do. Suppose to do. Want to Do. Should do. Expected to do. Would like to do. Unfinished tasks gnaw at us, growing like a hungry baby's wail inside our heads, depleting our energy and gnawing at our conscience. They drain our energy and cloud our spirit.

But I've found that I can stop the gnawing if I capture the tasks bouncing around my head.

Do that by getting them down on paper or into a computer file. Capture anything you're thinking about, anything you're needing to do, anything you're worried about doing or anything you're trying to remember to do or want to do someday. Put it down. Then set up a reminder system and the saved gnaw energy can be put into task completion.

TIP #21

Learn to Nibble

Nibbling is a cure (or at least a prophylactic) for procrastination, overwhelming projects, and pages of to-dos. Here's the concept: don't take big bites, take small nibbles.

When you nibble at something you make it disappear bit-by-bit in small chewable portions. The easiest way to nibble is to think: what is the next thing I need to do to move this forward? Not the next big thing (do taxes), but the next small thing (locate receipts). Once that's nibbled, then ask again, what's the next thing I need to do? (Organize receipts). Done. Next? (Update software).

Nibbles are typically 10-20 minutes. They fit perfectly between meetings when you only have thirty minutes before the next one. They work well as motivators when you're not in the mood to do something hard or time-consuming. Knock off a few nibbles and you'll be surprised how that gets you interested in accomplishing more.

When you think about an end product, it may seem overwhelming, but when you think about a nibble, that's easy. Start with nibbles. Fill in gaps with nibbles. And use nibbles to get your motivation going.

Want to be winning at working? Nibble. Nibble. Nibble.

ৡৡৡ

TIP #22

Think in Parallel

Increase your productivity and significantly impact your results by working parallel tracks, not linear ones.

Let me give you a personal example. I'm writing my next book, *Hitting Your Stride*. Currently, I have four parallel tracks going: (1) building an audience (platform); (2) writing the book; (3) developing promotional approaches; (4) learning more about the book business. I allocate time for each track each week, so by the time the book is published, #1, #3 and #4 will be developed to support its launch.

If I used a linear plan, waiting until I was finished writing the book to develop the audience and promotional approaches to augment the publisher's efforts, I would limit what would be possible under tight time constraints and significantly reduce my results.

Learn to look at the end goal, developing and working on parallel initiatives to bring that goal to fruition. Want to be winning at working? Work in parallel.

ഛഛഛ

"If people knew how hard I had to work to gain my mastery; it wouldn't seem so wonderful."
~ Michelangelo ~

TIP #23

Immoveable Deadlines

Why is it that a class reunion, a wedding, or a boss's work deadline gets us motivated to lose the ten pounds, plan the event or achieve the goal? It's an immoveable date.

So, one trick I've used to be winning at working is to create that same motivation by locking in dates, then doing the work. For example, rather than do the project work and then set the project deadline, I believe in doing it the other way. Set the date, then do the work. It's amazing how much you can get done when you have a deadline for achievement.

When I wanted to launch a new website, I hired the web designer, set and published the date for launch. It would have been easier to do the work and launch the site when it was ready. But, setting the goal made it happen quickly and on time. That way, we both made it a priority.

Napoleon Hill, author of *Think and Grow Rich*, put it this way, "Definiteness of purpose is the starting point of all achievement, and its lack is the stumbling block for ninety eight out of every one hundred people because they never really define their goals and start toward them."

Setting immoveable deadlines is a technique that can create personal and team motivation.

TIP #24

Finding Time

According to U.S. Census Bureau data, Americans spend more than 100 hours a year commuting to work.

That's 100 hours you can use for self-improvement. Granted it may come in 20 or 30 or 40 minute chunks. But it's time just for you. I've used my commuting time for over fifteen years (now we're talking cumulative hours) to listen to business books on tape. Books I wanted to read but couldn't find the time were easily digested commuting to work. And I learned how to do it at minimum expense. After I listen to the tapes, I resell them on eBay, recovering on average 60-70% of the original price.

You can even carry a pre-loaded MP3 player with winning at working or success oriented Podcasts, audio books or digital motivational downloads. Listen while you're waiting at the dentist's office, waiting for your child's soccer practice to end, doing your morning workout, walking the dog, mowing the lawn or commuting to work.

People who are winning at working devote time to self-improvement and increasing their knowledge. They creatively use their time.

ৼৼৼ

"Time is a created thing. To say 'I don't have time,'
is like saying 'I don't want to.'"
~ Lao-Tzu ~

TIP #25

Keeping Work in Perspective

What would happen if your work didn't get done today? Really, I mean it. What would happen?

For most of us, there are no life or death consequences. That's good to keep in mind. If we were hit by the proverbial beer-truck tomorrow, somehow work would manage to go on.

Perspective. Maybe, it's time to get some. You can make yourself crazy with the have-to-dos, need-to-dos, and should-dos.

Philosopher and mathematician, Bertrand Russell, offers this thought: "One of the symptoms of approaching nervous breakdown is the belief that one's work is terribly important. If I were a medical man, I should prescribe a holiday to any patient who considered his work important."

I find his words a good reminder.

೪೪೪

TIP #26

Take It or Leave It ... But Get It

We all need feedback. But remember feedback is opinion, not fact. It's something to evaluate, not blindly accept.

I find when several people have the same perception, it's good to listen. When I get insights I hadn't thought about, it's good to consider them. When input is mixed, it's good to follow my instincts. But when people provide feedback with a hatchet, finding only fault rather than offering ideas for improvement, it's good to look at it with distant curiosity.

Bottom line: if you want to be winning at working you must learn to seek and offer well-intentioned feedback. I think of it like the Sicilian proverb: "Only your real friends will tell you your face is dirty." Let input, suggestions, and feedback be real friends at work.

TIP #27

Live and Learn Days

I'm a detailed person, and I've learned to check and recheck. So when I heard about an issue that involved my brand (me!) and my winning at working website, I was first surprised, and then after investigating, alarmed.

Thanks to the person who gave me a heads-up, it was corrected in a few hours. But, it got me thinking. What we think we know, may not be right.

While I was upset about what happened I chose to view it as personal development, taking comfort in Thomas Blandi's words, "If you are not having problems, you are missing an opportunity for growth."

TIP #28

Step Out

Too often we default to our fears, letting them reign over life's opportunities. It's the fear that decides if we're interested in going for a new position, moving to a new city, changing careers, speaking to groups or learning new skills. It's the fear that hijacks our potential, stifles our growth and constrains us from winning at working.

Maybe you're afraid of failure or afraid of success, so you decide it's better to stay with what you know. Maybe you're afraid you'll be disappointed in your results so you cocoon yourself into comfort zone confinement. Maybe you're afraid you'll look foolish so you opt out of competing, or you're concerned you'll be found out as an imposter or disliked if you pursue your passions or step up to more responsibility.

It doesn't matter what our fears are or why we give them control. What matters is if we let them limit us; if we trade our comfort for our relevance and compromise our life's potential to eliminate that pit in our stomach. And if we do, it's no wonder we're not living our dreams.

You stay the same person if you keep doing the same things. Stepping outside your comfort zone is a conscious effort to stop your thoughts from stopping you. You're the one who gives your thoughts meaning.

People who are winning at working know stepping outside their comfort zone creates personal growth and development. They push themselves to do things that are "uncomfortable."

ఴఴఴ

"We are the choices we make."
~ Meryl Streep ~

TIP #29

You Have to Be Out There

Sitting in the bleachers, watching others, is not an option for people who want to be winning at working. You have to be out there, trying things, making mistakes, learning, growing and evolving. But being out there means dealing with the setbacks as well as the successes.

How you deal with your setbacks (big or small) will determine your long-term results. Failure is not the lack of success. Failure is staying down when you trip or stumble. It's giving up, checking out, or shutting down.

I wasn't a failure when I was fired from my first professional job, although for awhile I felt like one, and I could have been if I'd lost my confidence and given up on my career aspirations. I wasn't a failure when I was passed over for a coveted promotion I'd worked years for, but I could have been if I'd let that setback determine my future. And I wasn't a failure every time I pitched an idea that got turned down, but I could have been if I'd stopped pitching ideas.

How you view your disappointments, stumbles and falls will impact your future. Do you see them as stepping stones or brick walls? People who are winning at working live Ralph Waldo Emerson's words, "Men succeed when they realize that their failures are the preparation for their victories."

It's when you stop being out there that you stop making progress. And progress is what it's all about.

TIP #30

Ideas In – Ideas Out

I traveled from Montana to Texas to attend a seminar not in my field. I wasn't a candidate for the specific systems presented for establishing a referral real estate, mortgage lending, title, or home building business, but I'm always a candidate for learning. So, I decided to accompany my daughter-in-law, who was, at the time, in the mortgage lending business, to see what ideas the conference might generate. It was a highly productive experience.

You see, seeds of ideas are everywhere and as long as you're putting new thoughts, concepts, information and perspectives in, you keep getting new thoughts, concepts and perspectives out. I've found, some of the most powerful ideas come from the least expected places.

ৎৎৎ

INSIGHT

Check Your Thoughts

It was clear she was having "one of those days." But to be truthful, I didn't care. I was too nervous about my surgery to pay attention to Doris, the nurse grousing about how overworked she was that Thursday. But by the time I was wheeled back to my same-day surgical room, she was even less hospitable and more entrenched in complaining.

So, I was surprised when a young nurse introduced herself and said that she was called in to help. You'd think it would have made Doris happy to have assistance. But to the contrary, it exacerbated the situation. She barked at me when she discovered "that other nurse" had taken out my IV, as if I had directed the action.

Doris was focused on Doris. It was her routine, her systems, her hospital wing that was disrupted by too many patients and a new staff member. It was her day that was complicated by additional help. And it was her to-do list that I was on.

My Doris experience got me thinking. It wasn't poor customer-focus that caused her behavior. It was deeper than that. It was poor thought-focus. Doris viewed the additional nurse as a hindrance, not a help; a burden which only added to her thoughts of being a victim. Constrained by woe-is-me thinking, she concentrated on the disruption to her, not the bigger purpose of enhanced patient care. No amount of support would have changed Doris' day. It was her mind-set, not her work-load that triggered her reaction.

There are plenty of overworked people. It's the norm in workplaces to have more to do than time to do it. That's not going to change. But how you approach your mountain of work is a choice. Do you water your frustrations, irritations and "poor-me" thinking, like Doris, or do you yank out those thoughts, replacing them with a commitment to tackle each task, one at a time, offering the best of who you are to the issues confronting you?

You see, it's not the work that drowns us, it's our thinking. Our thoughts determine our reality. As American philosopher William James put it, "The greatest discovery of my generation is that human beings, by changing the inner attitudes of their minds, can change the outer aspects of their lives."

It may have been the greatest discovery of his generation a hundred years ago, but we need to rediscover it for ours. People who are winning at working understand the correlation between what they think and what they get. They're aware of their thoughts, consciously choosing ones that work for them, not against them.

If you think yourself a victim, you'll act the part. But if you think yourself a problem-solver, you'll figure things out. If you think your work is difficult, you won't be disappointed. But if you enjoy a challenge, you'll find yourself engaged. If you think your boss is an idiot, she'll live up to your expectations. But if you find her thought-provoking, your perception alters. *You* decide what thoughts fill your day. Want to be winning at working? Check your thoughts.

ഔഔഔ

"There's a powerful connection between the words we use and the results we get."
.~ Nan S. Russell ~

TIP #31

Power Your Future

I'm a quotation lover. I collect them. I read them. I use them to inspire me, to challenge my thinking and to guide my thoughts. This is one of my personal favorites:

"It is not your environment; it is you – the quality of your mind, the integrity of your soul, the determination of your will – that will decide your future and shape your life."
~ Benjamin E. Mays ~

Are your thoughts limiting or invigorating? Self-restricting or self-empowering? Think it's impossible and you'll build your own walls. Think you can't and you set yourself up for a self-fulfilling result. Think you can and your thinking can help make it happen.

Years ago, I told a friend about a promotion that would take me from what I knew into a new discipline. She quickly responded, "How could you say yes? You won't know what you're doing." It surprised me. I'd never thought of saying anything other than yes. "I'll figure it out," I told her. And I did.

My thinking told me I could figure things out. Her thinking told her she couldn't. That difference played out in our careers.

There's power in your thoughts. Power to bring results, create realities and banish walls. Power to overcome challenges, eliminate barriers and achieve what others only dream. Want to be winning at working? Power your thoughts to positively impact *your* future.

TIP #32

Watch Yourself

According to Aristotle, "We are what we repeatedly do." I agree, and it can have both positive and not so positive consequences.

Take time and watch yourself. You acquire a habit by constantly acting in a particular way. Some are good ways; some are self-defeating. I have my share of both, but I've learned the value of checking-in to "watch" what I'm doing from time-to-time.

Recently I observed one of my habits was to immediately write down something that I find interesting. I've found it a helpful way to develop writing material and, since I'm a writer, that's a good habit. It's one to keep.

But I also identified a non-productive habit I'm in the process of developing. I noticed I pile things. So I have piles (not files). Now I can consciously work on correcting it.

Make time to step outside yourself on occasion and watch your behavior. What are you repeating? What habits are you developing that you like? Don't like? If you become what you repeatedly do, make sure it's the things you want to be doing.

ക്കൈ

"Everyone thinks of changing the world,
no one thinks of changing himself."
~ Leo Tolstoy ~

TIP #33

Read the Tea Leaves

To survive and thrive at work, you need to hone your tea leaf reading skills. Learning primarily through hindsight might work if you like being a Monday morning quarterback, but that approach is as helpful as my refrigerator magnet's counsel that "mistakes are part of the dues one pays for a full life." Sure, they are. But who needs an insightful reminder that you can't change the past.

What we need is a way to change our future. That's where reading tea leaves come in. Your goal should be to affect what is to come. You can't change how you've done, but you can change how you will do. Your future work-life is about the choices you still have to make. Read the tea leaves by learning to connect the dots and see the big picture and you'll make better choices at work.

TIP #34

Find People Touchstones

I'm indebted in my career to people who have been (and who currently are) touchstones for me. According to Webster, touchstones are used to determine "the quality or genuineness of a thing."

People touchstones are hard to find, but you'll know them for their candor. They're the ones not working a personal agenda. They're the ones who have your best interests at heart, who are able to see the big picture and are comfortable offering their no-strings attached perspectives. And they're the ones telling you the truth as they see it, who are willing to pull you back from the edge or push you out of a do-loop.

People touchstones keep you grounded, "real" and able to offer the best of who you are through your work. We all need that kind of help. Being a touchstone and having people act as touchstones for you, enables you to gain insights to be winning at working.

TIP #35

Like What You Do

The biggest index for success is this: find something you love to do. If you do, you will do it well.

Like Albert Schweitzer put it, "Success is not the key to happiness. Happiness is the key to success. If you love what you are doing you will be successful."

You can't be winning at working if you don't like what you're doing, where you're doing it, or who you're doing it for. If what you do feels like work the majority of the time, think about why, and what you can do to change it.

TIP #36

Tell 'Em Why

Driving from Montana to Colorado to visit family, we stopped for lunch at a well-known fast-food eatery to grab something to take with us. With only a few people in line, we figured we'd be back on the road shortly. Wrong.

Turns out the manager was training a new employee on the assembly-line process of putting sandwiches together. We've all been a new employee at some point, so everyone in line was patient as she took him through the process again and again.

But, he couldn't get it. With every sandwich he started, he made exactly the same mistakes. Not because he wasn't capable, but because she never told him *why* he should do certain things, certain ways.

You see, without the *why*, the what makes little sense. So, if you want to help others be winning at working, explain the reason behind the action. Not only will it expedite training, it will save time, increase consistency and impact results.

TIP #37

How Many Minds Have You Read Today?

None, I'd imagine.

Yet, if you're like me, sometimes I'm waiting for people to read mine ... waiting for my boss to know I want that new assignment; or my colleague to know I was irritated about his statement in the meeting and I'd like an apology; or my assistant to know I'd like her to answer my phone before the third ring ... or ... you get the point.

Waiting for someone to read your mind is like waiting for the goose to lay a golden egg. It only happens in fairy tales.

If you want someone to know what you're thinking, tell them. If getting the assignment is important to you, say so. If you're irritated with a colleague invite him for coffee and discuss it. If you want a different performance standard from a staff member, tell her. Mind reading is not a winning at working strategy, nor is waiting for someone to read yours.

TIP #38

Show, Don't Tell

People who talk about what they're going to do, what they'd like to do, or what they're thinking of doing someday are common in the workplace.

People who do what they say they're going to do, are not.

If you want to be winning at working be like a good novelist who shows, not tells. Successful people are doers.

సాసాసా

TIP #39

Schedule Self-Appointments

One of the first things I do with any new idea or project is schedule time on my calendar, setting aside two hour blocks one to three days a week, or perhaps a half day a week. I consider this appointment with myself as critical as any other on my schedule.

Scheduling dedicated time to think, plan, analyze, and move ideas and projects ahead positively impacts both productivity and results.

TIP #40

Clean Sweep Those Inner Files

If you happen to be working between Christmas and New Years, it's the perfect time to clean out files, delete emails and organize your office. Use this period of relatively quiet downtime to catch up on left-over tasks that never made it to the top of your priority list.

But more importantly, it's a good time to do a clean sweep of what's cluttered on the inside, too ... old patterns, habits, and critical self-talk.

TIP #41

Assess Your Progress

At the end of each year, it's a good time to assess what you've accomplished in the past twelve months from various vantage points: personal, professional, financial, and developmental.

I find it helpful to brainstorm what I've achieved in the past twelve months so I can look at the list and view my progress. Things often evolve slowly and unless I take time to see what's changed, I miss the progress I've made.

Some questions to think about:

1. What am I doing today that I wasn't doing a year ago?
2. What more do I know? In what areas have I grown?
3. Where did I go outside my comfort zone?
4. What skills have I acquired this past year?
5. What do I feel good about?

Take a minute to pat yourself on the back. Then take a few more minutes to write specific goals for next year.

၉၀၉၀၉၀

*"Better to do something imperfectly
than nothing flawlessly."*
~ Robert Schuller ~

TIP #42

One Idea a Day

One idea a day is all it takes to develop a creative thinking habit with big paybacks. You have hundreds of ideas passing through your head on any given day. The key is to recognize them and note them down. These are not world changing ideas I'm talking about, but the everyday type. Think of it more like idea-singles vs. idea-home runs, knowing that overtime singles can add up and be a winning strategy.

I keep online logs of ideas and add to them throughout the day, when something pops to mind or I come across something I find interesting. It may just be an idea snippet, but I still note it down. These lists include all sorts of things: potential column topics, enhancements for my website, marketing ideas for my book, personal development areas, or even fun weekend get-aways.

Often I have no idea what I'm going to do with the idea, but I find if I note it down I can come back to the list and cherry pick the best ideas, or evolve a snippet of an idea into something bigger and better.

Sometimes ideas are borrowed from others, or built on from other ones. Maybe I read something interesting that someone else is doing that's helped them, and that leads to an idea on how I might do something similar.

Ideas are everywhere. But, practicing a discipline to capture, develop and use them can dramatically impact your results.

TIP #43

Become A Quotation Lover

I love quotes. Good ones, that is. I collect them, and if you've ever been to any of my websites:

www.nanrussell.com

www.intheschemeofthings.com

www.winningatworking.com

you'll find collected favorites.

A good quote crystallizes thinking, offers nuggets of wisdom, or nudges me towards new areas of consideration. I know I've stumbled over one when I feel a truth within it touching me at a core level.

Start reading one quote a day and you'll discover an ongoing source of inspiration, reflection or motivation to keep you moving in the direction of your dreams. You'll discover enhanced creativity and new insights for handling your work and your life. And you'll awaken the passion and talents you have to offer the world.

You can have a daily quotation delivered to your email or cell phone (my site, www.dailyworkvitamin.com, is one possibility). Or get a book of quotations, leave it by the side of your bed, and read one before you get up every morning. You'll be surprised what becoming a quotation lover will do for you.

৶৶৶

"Years may wrinkle the skin, but to give up enthusiasm wrinkles the soul."
~ Samuel Ullmann ~

TIP #44

Invest in You

One way you can develop your talent is by investing in yourself. Sometimes that investment may be a monetary one: attending a seminar; taking a class; buying and listening to motivational tapes; using a personal coach. If you're interesting in a winning at working coach, you'll find my program, *Winning Ways*, helpful. Sometimes the self-investment is time: practicing, taking a "think week" like Bill Gates, reading, meditating, or exercising,

You see, the more you invest in you, the more you'll develop your talents and abilities and the more return you'll get. People who are winning at working invest in growing their talents. They know Emerson was right when he said, "No one can cheat you out of ultimate success but yourself."

৽৽৽

TIP #45

Learn to Write

When I first began my career twenty-something years ago, writing skills didn't matter as much. Now with email as a primary communication method, they're critical. Poorly written emails cause more than confusion. They cause unnecessary irritation and misdirected efforts.

Learn to write well. Make your written communications simple, concise and clear.

With today's business world's reliance on email, writing is a critical performance skill. Honing your writing skills will help you differentiate your performance and your results.

TIP #46

Put Your Name to Your Work

I noticed a difference taking classes in an online format where students post their work and offer their point-of-view in a class discussion log for everyone to read.

I found the comments more thoughtful, insightful, and connected to the material than those blurted out in college classrooms. To me the difference was that one's name was permanently attached to one's comments. I know I was more thoughtful before I entered my perspectives on those assignment boards.

Remember first grade when we proudly printed our names so everyone could see them at the top of that wide-ruled paper? A few of the best papers ended up plastered to the classroom walls for all to see.

We may not write our names in big, bold crayon letters on our work anymore, but make no mistake, our name is *in* the work we do.

TIP #47

Learn and Practice Your Craft

I spent three days with eleven other writers in an immersion fiction writing workshop.

Writers' conferences draw some want-to-be writers who believe they can write the next million dollar best seller. Maybe some can. But, for most of us, writing is like most things in life. Even if you have a little talent, getting good takes practice and hard work. And if you want to be really good, you have to practice every day.

It's no different if you want to be a good athlete, musician, or business person. Building your skills should be an all the time focus. If you want to be winning at working, think about what you can do to learn new skills, practice those skills and develop *your craft* everyday.

ço ço ço

TIP #48

Pay Attention to Little Things on Your Resume

When we pick fresh fruits and vegetables, we select out ones that are wilted, with blemishes or irregularities. We select in those that are fresh, inviting, and blemish free.

The same is true with resumes. As a hiring manager sifting through hundreds and hundreds of resumes, the first thing I'd do was narrow the pile by eliminating as many as possible. I'd select *out*, not *in*, and any little reason would do it - misspellings, poor presentation, untargeted response.

Little blemishes cause fruit and resumes to both be rejected.

TIP #49

Don't Even Think About Pushing SEND!

Angry after a meeting? Frustrated with that voice mail? Irritated with an email you just got? Tempted to write back your strong point of view to set the record straight?

Okay. Go ahead. Write it. Get it out of your system – vent, rage, argue, or whatever you need to do. Then save it to read later for laughs, or delete it. Don't even think about pushing that send button. The light bulb in your head should be blinking red: Stop – potential career damage ahead. Stop. Stop.

Better yet – pick up the phone or walk down the hall and see the person. Face to face or live over the phone is a better solution in these cases. Email is a permanent record and often escalates a situation.

INSIGHT

Changing Rules

Poor Pluto. Stripped of its planetary status by the International Astronomical Union and reclassified as a "dwarf planet," Pluto's demotion heralds new rules for planet classification. A week of debate by renowned astronomers from seventy-five countries culminated in the decision to reduce the number of planets to eight "classic" ones.

This reclassification got me thinking. Like a company reorganization or leadership change, the rules were altered. And no matter if you were among scientists advocating for more planets or less, it no longer matters. The decision is rendered. Like it. Don't like it. It's done.

Organizational changes can be like that too. Like Pluto, I've spent career years with "classic" designation, status and access only to be "reclassified" with mergers, acquisitions, downsizing and reorganizations. Confident, comfortable and courageous with a current boss, you must re-prove, readjust and reorient to a new one with a different style, focus and rules.

It's happened enough in my career-life to collect a few insights along the way. First, the suddenness is unnerving and often painful. Familiar shifts to unfamiliar and second-nature decisions become second-guessed ones. When the rules change it's uncomfortable.

But, you can't go back. You can't change the outcome. What was true yesterday is gone. So, my second lesson learned the hard way is let it go as quickly as possible. Your future depends on it. Third, recognize you're in a growth spurt. That can be painful, challenging or exhilarating. And while it might not be a growth you'd choose, use your talent to reinvent yourself, find your grounding and contribute in new ways.

You see, if change can happen to something as sure as planets, it will likely happen to us. When it does, we can dig in, resist and fight, or, after taking a deep breath and regrouping, we can find our courage and take a step forward.

That's what people who are winning at working do. They choose the future over the past, personal growth over fossilization, opportunity over defeat and contribution over consternation. And as difficult as that is at times to do, people who are winning at working work through their disappointments and wounds, assessing their options, inventing their future and finding their wisdom. Like an African proverb reminds us all, "When the music changes, so does the dance."

ço·ço·ço

*"If we did all the things we are capable of doing, we
would literally astound ourselves."*
~ Thomas Edison ~

TIP #50

The Credit Doesn't Matter

Some people get hung up on who is going to get the credit. Others withhold ideas for fear someone will steal them, as if there is a shortage of their creative thoughts. Still others let their ego get in the way of their results.

One piece of advice my father gave me about business was that it's better to give away ideas, suggestions, and information. It's better to let someone else take the credit than not get something done. It's better to focus on results.

You see, ultimately whatever you give away comes back to you. Maybe not today or tomorrow, but over time. In business, as in life, you get what you give.

Benjamin Jowett, a nineteenth century scholar put it this way, "The way to get things done is not to mind, who gets the credit of doing them."

I couldn't agree more.

TIP #51

What You Know, When You Know It

Don't wait to package information. Effective communication is timely. Keep bosses, staff and peers in the loop on issues that pertain to their responsibilities. That includes the good news and the not so good.

In less than a minute, a phone call, email, voice mail or text message can alert people to direction changes, emerging problems, new perspectives or meeting results. People can filter what they don't need, but not knowing critical information is a trust-buster.

People who are winning at working use active communication practices as a cornerstone for enhancing relationships, building trust, and impacting results.

TIP #52

Deliver

There's one talent that defines people who are winning at working. They don't disappoint. They deliver. They consistently produce what they say they will. And they do it again and again and again.

People who are winning at working deliver what they promise. If anything they *under*-promise and *over*-deliver, without ever sandbagging. Every time they do what they say they're going to do, they build their credibility. And credibility builds careers.

TIP #53

It's Not the Drum

"He who cannot dance will say: the drum is bad." Too many people use a philosophy akin to this African proverb to navigate their work. It's easier to blame the drum or the boss, the co-worker or the company. Easier to criticize the workload, the training or lack of it, the pay or one's upbringing. And easier to fault anything and everyone rather than their own actions, choices, and results.

Every time you offer excuses, blame something or point fingers at someone, you give away your power and control. Every time you don't attempt to solve the problem because it's difficult, you fortify a can't do mind set. And every time you waste time pinpointing who did what wrong, instead of improving the process or training or communicating so it won't happen again, you trade future for past.

People who are winning at working are self-reflective. They see themselves as accountable to themselves for offering the best of who they are, despite poor bosses, uncooperative co-workers, less than optimal conditions or challenging roadblocks. They create their own pockets of excellence where they can "dance." And, if in fact they finally determine that the drum is indeed a bad drum, they still don't blame it. They figure out how to get a good one.

TIP #54

Take a Time Out

When young children misbehave, many parents, teachers and caregivers insist on a time-out. Think how much better your workplace would be if you initiated the same approach. No, not for your boss or coworkers, but for yourself.

People who are winning at working use this approach. They self-monitor to determine when they need to step back. They recognize that do-loop debating, trench-dug positions and hot tempers are not conducive to enhanced decision making, creativity or positive work relationships. Not to mention that people stop listening. They know the adult equivalent of a temper-tantrum is not quickly forgotten in the workplace, and unprofessional antics can derail a career.

When you feel like you're teetering on the edge or spinning toward unproductive emotions, initiate a time-out. You don't have to call it that, but take a walk around the building, shut your office door, get a cup of coffee, or suggest the group get back together later to continue the discussion.

જ⊷જ⊷જ

*"Your emotions tell you
what your soul wants you to know."*
~ Gary Zukav ~

TIP #55

Progress, Not Perfection

It's action, not inaction, practice not theory, and progress not perfection that builds success, achieves results and actualizes dreams.

After hearing me speak at a conference, a young woman sought me out. She was struggling with this concept of progress not perfection, and asked for advice. "How do you do it?" she asked. "How do you accept something as finished when you know it could be better?" She proceeded to tell me that she was managing a project that was over budget and nine months past the deadline. Her boss had made his displeasure clear. Yet, she struggled. "If only I had more time to do it right," she pined.

There's a difference between doing *your best under the circumstances,* and trying to achieve perfection. Whatever our work, we must move it forward to get results. Our work is a work in progress. And so are we.

So unlike many who spend their days trying to make something perfect, people who are winning at working spend their days making progress. Making progress, any progress, fuels their motivation, creativity and energy. It builds their momentum. And it ignites their results.

TIP #56

What Can You Do for Me Today?

It is a what have you done today world. A congratulations and a thank you for saving the project from certain ruin last week; getting an outstanding review; developing a new product line; meeting your budget; working all weekend to deliver the boss's requested information; and countless other things. Feel Good. Be Happy. Move On. If I'm your boss, I have. Now, I'm wondering what you can do today.

"While wishing and hoping makes you a dreamer, acting and doing makes you someone who can turn dreams into reality."
~ Nan S. Russell ~

INSIGHT

Someone Else

My friend, Beth Pelkofsky, who helped orchestrate and edit this little book of tips, was the impetus behind the column below that I wrote as part of my Winning at Working column series, www.winningatworking.com.

Perhaps more than any other winning philosophy, this one lays a cornerstone for nibbling your way to success. So, I thought it appropriate to end with Beth's story.

"I'm sorry, but I have to vent. It was a horrible day at work," began my friend on our monthly catch-up call. "We've all been there," I offered. "Yeah, but not like this." As a substitute instructional aid, she'd been asked to assist teachers on a field trip for 275 fifth graders to celebrate the successful completion of a testing week. Her bus was the last unloaded and by the time she entered the skating rink, it was chaos.

Teachers were standing, arms crossed, griping that no one from the administration was there to organize the event; no one told them what was suppose to happen; and no one had alerted the rink to their coming. While all legitimate concerns, being angry, frustrated and absorbed in their own plight meant no one was dealing with scores of eleven-year-olds rushing to grab skates, ripping open snacks, pushing to get sodas and throwing trash on the floor.

"I was utterly horrified," my friend told me. After watching for several minutes, she decided to recruit a teacher and the two of them began organizing students and assigning tasks to teachers. She did what people who are winning at working do. They act.

In twenty years in management, I've seen people waiting, watching and hoping someone else would step up, take ownership and make things happen. I've seen people stuck in blame-gear while others are doing the work and solving the problems. And I've seen people hesitating while others are committing. No surprise these were the same people complaining in my office when others received bigger increases, better assignments, or more interesting projects.

You see, people who are winning at working become the someone else that others are waiting for. They step up and do something. They know when to act, and they feel better about themselves when they do. That's because action feels better than inaction and commitment feels better than non-commitment. Both build your self-esteem.

So, here's my bottom-line: you can't be winning at working if you're waiting for someone else to be the someone you could be. In my way of thinking, winning at working means you commit to offering the best you there is. Sometimes that means you have to dig a little deeper for your courage or push yourself outside your comfort zone. Sometimes it means you have to handle 275 out of control children when you're the lowest ranking person around. But it's like Shakespeare said, "Nothing comes from doing nothing."

ABOUT THE AUTHOR

From minimum wage employee to Vice President of $4.4 billion dollar QVC, Nan S. Russell knows what it takes to survive and thrive in this what-have-you-done-for-me-today world. From roles transforming a corporate culture to heading a new subsidiary, the launch of which was reported in both the *Wall Street Journal* and *USA Today*, she offers real-world experience with a motivational and business context.

Nan has spent over twenty years in management and knows both sides of the desk. She's held leadership positions in Human Resources, Communication, Marketing and line Management. She was the architect and influence leader of a culture transformation for 10,000 employees. Nan has a B.A. from Stanford University and M.A. from the University of Michigan.

In 2002, Nan left the corporate world to pursue a life-dream to work and write from the mountains of northwestern Montana. Today she is a successful author, consultant, coach and speaker completing her new book, *Hitting Your Stride.*

Her syndicated career insights column, *Winning at Working* (www.winningatworking.com) appears in over eighty publications, and her life-reflections column, *In the Scheme of Things* (www.intheschemeofthings.com) is published in six states and Canada, and appears in several anthologies including *Chicken Soup for the Shopper's Soul, Cup of Comfort for Weddings, Classic Christmas* and *Letters to My Teacher.*

Nan S. Russell is President of MountainWorks Communications LLC, a company she founded in 2006 to support her passion for helping organizations build winning work cultures, and helping people bring the best of who they are to the world, realize their dreams and live their life's potential.

Learn more about Nan and her work at www.nanrussell.com; contact at info@nanrussell.com.

Do You Want to Get Better Results and Advance Your Career – With Less Effort?

And Get Paid More at Work in the Process?

If so, discover more winning philosophies and real-world career insights to help you live your life's potential:

➢ **Free eColumn subscription** to *Winning at Working* www.winningatworking.com

➢ **Free Podcast subscription** to *Winning at Working* www.winningatworking.com

➢ **Inspiration on the Go.** Receive a daily dose of inspiration on your cell phone each morning www.DailyWorkVitamin.com

➢ **Want to be coached by Nan?** Learn about her individual and group Winning Coaching Programs www.MountainWorksCommunications.com

➢ **Want Nan to speak to your organization?** www.nanrussell.com

➢ **More *Winning at Working* Products and Services** www.MountainWorksCommunications.com

For more information visit: www.nanrussell.com

We hope you enjoyed *Nibble Your Way to Success: 56 Winning Tips for Taking Charge of Your Career.*

If you or your company or organization is interested in purchasing additional copies of this book at a **group rate**, contact us at info@MountainWorksPress.com

Hitting Your Stride

Nan S. Russell

Capital Books   January 2008